El Corazón y la Muerte

Curated by Kikyz1313

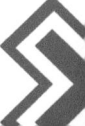

Published by GalleryX, a division of Adverbage Ltd., 65 South William Street, Dublin 2, Ireland.
www.galleryx.ie.

The illustrations *El Último Canto* and *Idolo de Juguete* are © 2016 Alejandro Barrón; used by permission.
The illustrations *El Corazón y la Muerte* and *Forever Young* are © 2016 Rodrigo Cifuentes; used by permission.
The illustrations *Testigo* and *Untitled* are © 2016 Mario Cinquemani; used by permission.
The illustrations *Cyan* and *Luz Perpetua* are © 2016 Ricardo Fernandez; used by permission.
The illustrations *Untitled* and *Play* are © 2016 Victor Hugo Jácome; used by permission.
The illustrations *Amor y Miedo* and *Cabeza de Santo* are © 2016 José Luis López Galván; used by permission.
The illustration *Lucky Charms* is © 2016 Patrick Mallow; used by permission.
The illustrations *Empty Whispers I* and *Empty Whispers II* are © 2016 Román Miranda; used by permission.
The illustrations *Obituario I*, *Obituario II*, and *Obituario III* are © 2016 Rafael Rodríguez; used by permission.
The illustrations *Quiebre y Mayólica* and *Ablación* are © 2016 Rolando Sosa; used by permission.
The illustrations *Flyman* and *Metallic Taste* are © 2016 Talía Yañez; used by permission.
The illustration *True Love Shredded by Conflict* is © 2016 Kikyz1313; used by permission.

First edition 2016.

A catalogue record for this book is available from the British Library.

ISBN-10 0-9541723-9-6
ISBN-13 978-0-9541723-9-8

Cover illustration: *Cabeza de Santo* by José Luis López Galván.

Printed and bound by LightningSource.

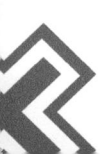

Since they became self-aware and started looking for meaning in their short lives, humans have deliberately fought against the passage of time. They have devoted all their ingenuity, inventiveness and heart to challenging Death.

Art, this cathartic instrument of our emotions, evokes all that broadens and enriches the spirit. Most of all, however, it purges that which blackens our minds and numbs our hearts: the unknown, the unusual, and the terrifying reminder of the fragility of our existence.

Clearly, this exhibition is not trying to avoid these feelings. If we exorcised our fears, we would simply cloud and impede the evolution of our species. Nor is it trying to achieve senseless entertainment or simple decoration. This project wants to describe, and show the world, the cruel beauty of the duality of our existence, its fragile and less known side: our fascination with death.

There is something hidden and yet attractive about death. It's a curious call that is always striving to solve the eternal mystery of our purpose in this world. In Mexican culture specifically, mystery and mourning almost become a celebration of life, where the two extremes of existence find a balance, because instead of trying to escape or deny their destiny, Mexicans maintain profound respect for the eventualities of life.

This vision of life and death is unique in the world and, at the same time, it forges Mexican artists' unique understanding of and affinity with the macabre, an understanding that produces exceptional art that is, however, little known in the rest of the world.

El Corazón y la Muerte wants to open a dialogue of cultural and intellectual interchange between Mexican contemporary culture and the rest of the world, with Ireland as a starting point. Twelve well-known emerging artists from Mexico will perform a cathartic representation of unique reflections on the macabre and the unusual, between life and death.

By showcasing traditional techniques like painting and drawing at an exquisite level of craftsmanship, together with transcendental concepts and ideas, *El Corazón y la Muerte* promises to be an exhibition of a calibre rarely found in international art circles nowadays.

— Kikyz1313

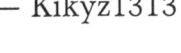

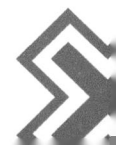

Alejandro Barrón

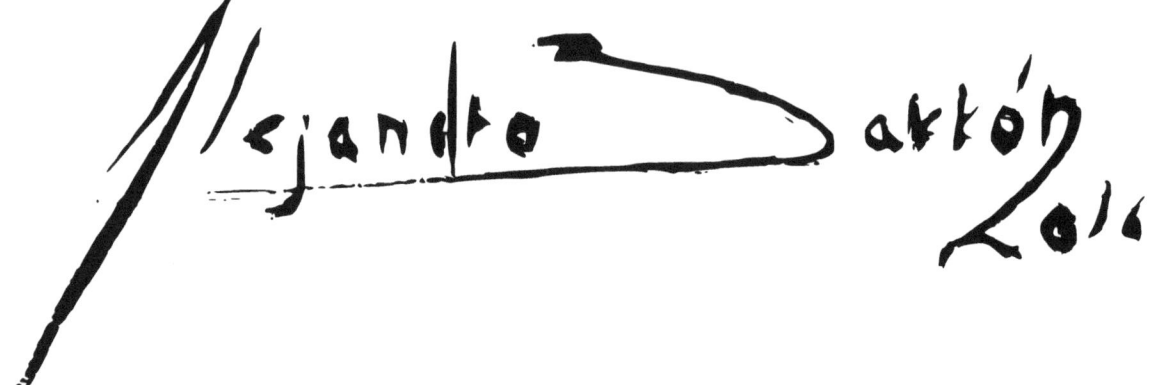

Born in Mexico City, 1980, Alejandro first specialized in lithography at the National School of Fine Arts (ENAP) and later trained himself in the art of life painting by strict observation and bold persistence. This led to his first solo show in 2007 at the Centro Cultural San Ángel. In 2013, the artist started his foray into international art circles with Meyer Gallery, New Mexico. Alejandro has quickly gained recognition and has exhibited his artworks in over 35 group exhibitions and 10 solo shows in Mexico and internationally. Most of his works are part of major private and public art collections around the globe such as Grupo Milenio, Miguel Bañuls Ribas (Spain), Universidad Autónoma de Chapingo and many others.

Alejandro's artworks are usually transformed depictions of the living and the motionless; figures corrupted by time, diseased, neglected, forgotten or over-used, but renovated with precise emotional and aesthetic proportions that drive us to the true acknowledgement of the object as itself: to re-perceive the horrific, the visceral, the erotic, the naked body, the portrait, the animal, the forgotten child's toy, the found bones results in a wholly new visual possibility, and the appreciation of those tiny details we tend to overlook in our vain day-by-day existence.

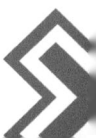

Alejandro Barrón: *El Último Canto (The Last Song)*
Oil on paper, 50 x 40 cm

"This painting represents the absence of love due to the emotional or affective inability to feel. The human relic that appears in this painting has a residual gesture of pain, which can be even perceived as indifference. Moths surround the hands and chest as a symbol of a love in agony, lost in the wind, in an empty place, a melody that no one recalls any more as it has been lost in the depths of memory, the last breath of life. Only this mummified gesture lasts as the final memory of himself."

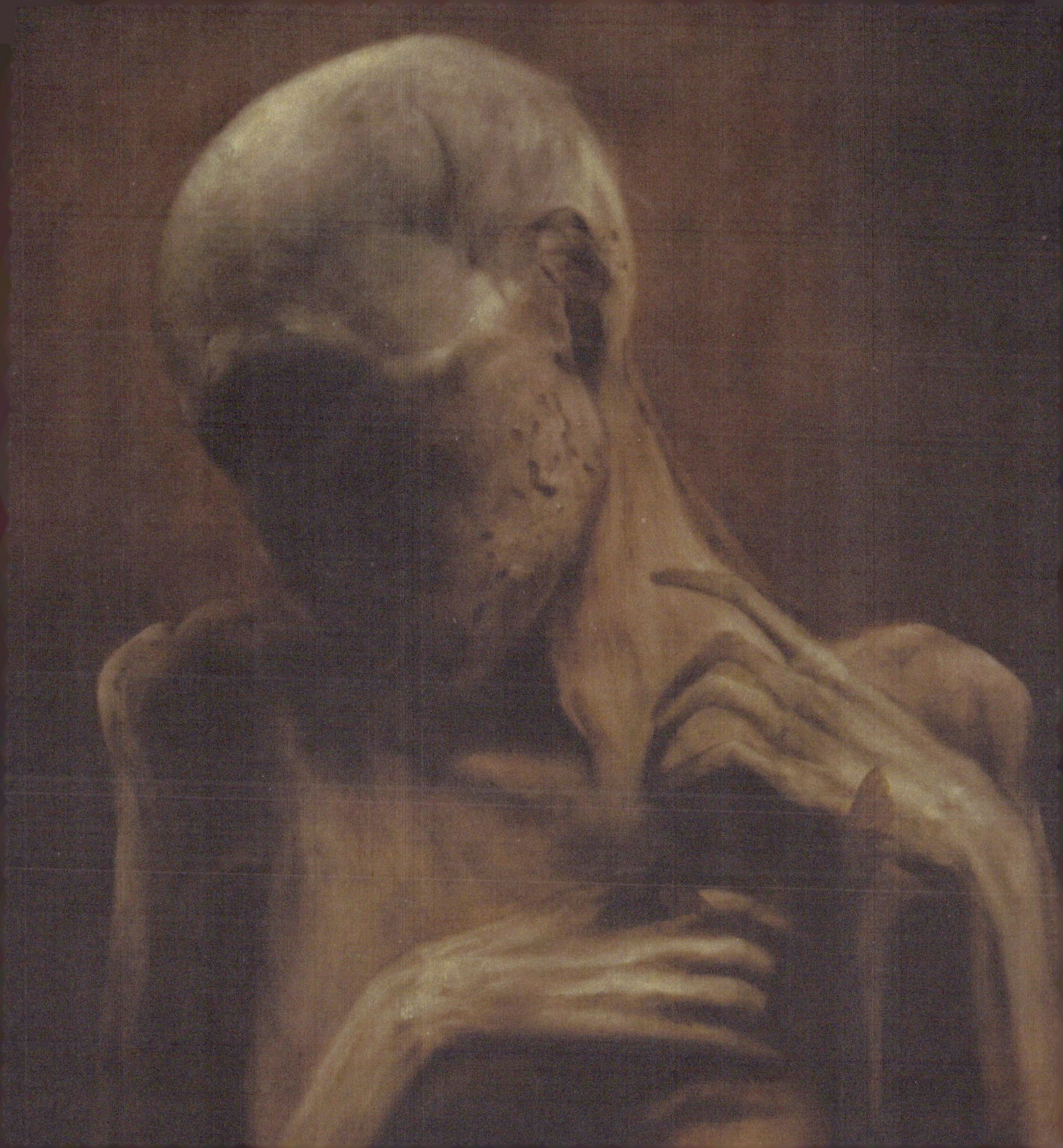

Alejandro Barrón: *Idolo de Juguete (Toy Idol)*
Oil on paper, 50 x 40 cm

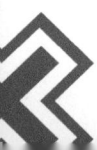

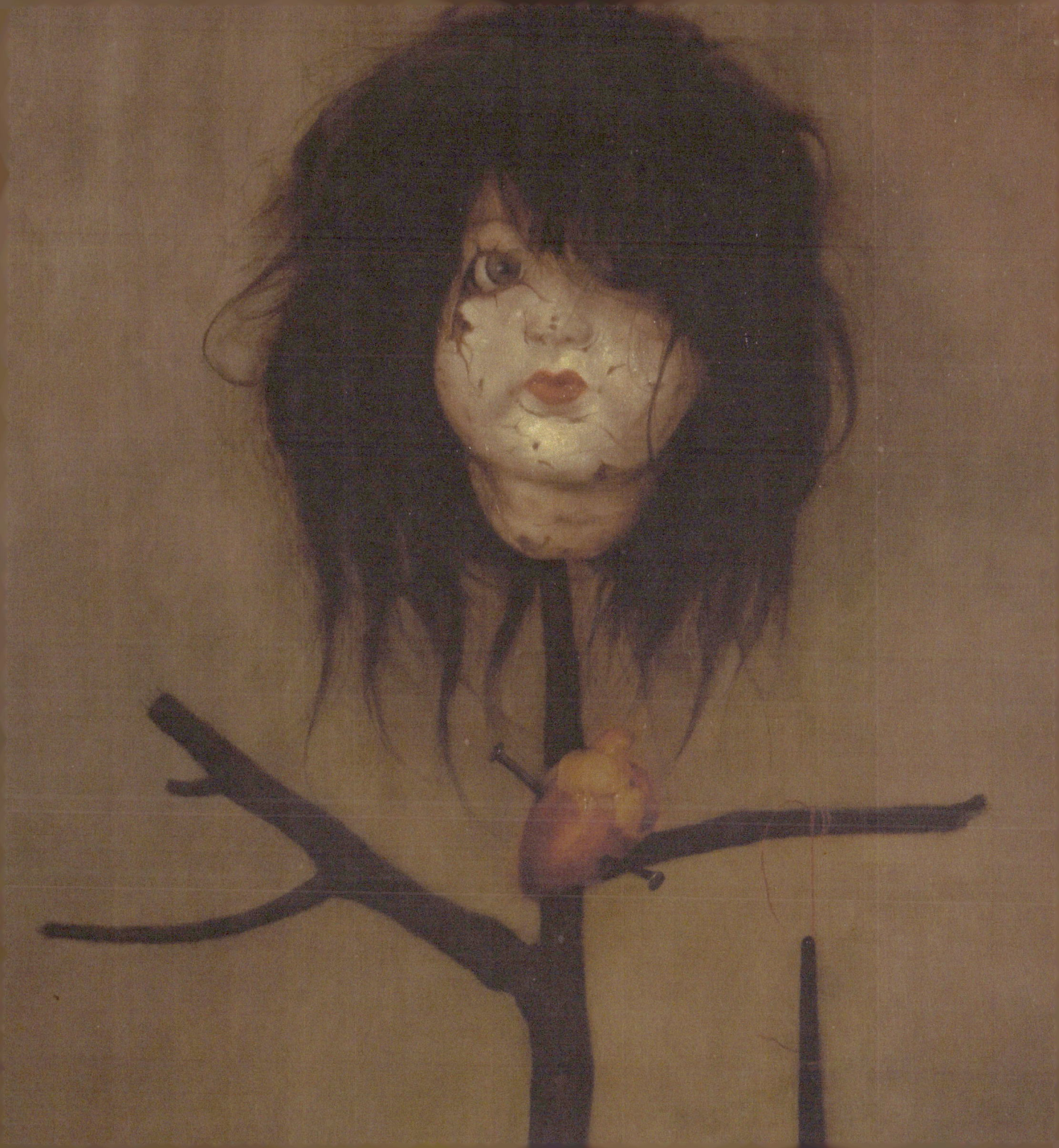

Rodrigo Cifuentes

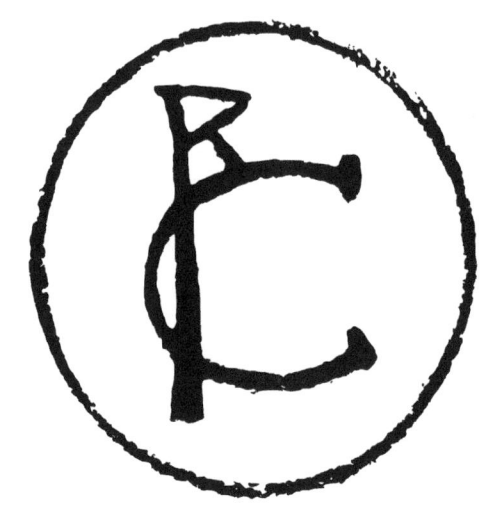

Born in Jalisco, Mexico, in 1980, Rodrigo is a descendant of refugees from the Spanish Civil War of 1930. He grew up in a violent environment that shaped his pictorial character, which he developed later at the National School of Painting, Sculpture and Printmaking La Esmeralda (ENPEG) in Mexico City. He resides in Querétaro City, where he's currently developing his work.

Rodrigo is a tenebrist contemporary painter by vocation: through his paintings he analyses the dichotomy of the Latin American myth and the American dream in his society. The deafening presence of an expressionist scream speaks to that social discontent, approaching such subjects as the unreachability of the American dream, loss of innocence, and mass consumption.

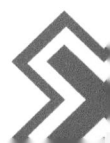

Rodrigo Cifuentes: *El Corazón y la Muerte (Death and the Heart)*
Oil on board, 30 x 30 cm

"Create images leaving aside concept over intellectualization, as simple as dancing to Alphaville's beat."

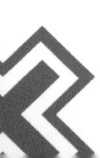

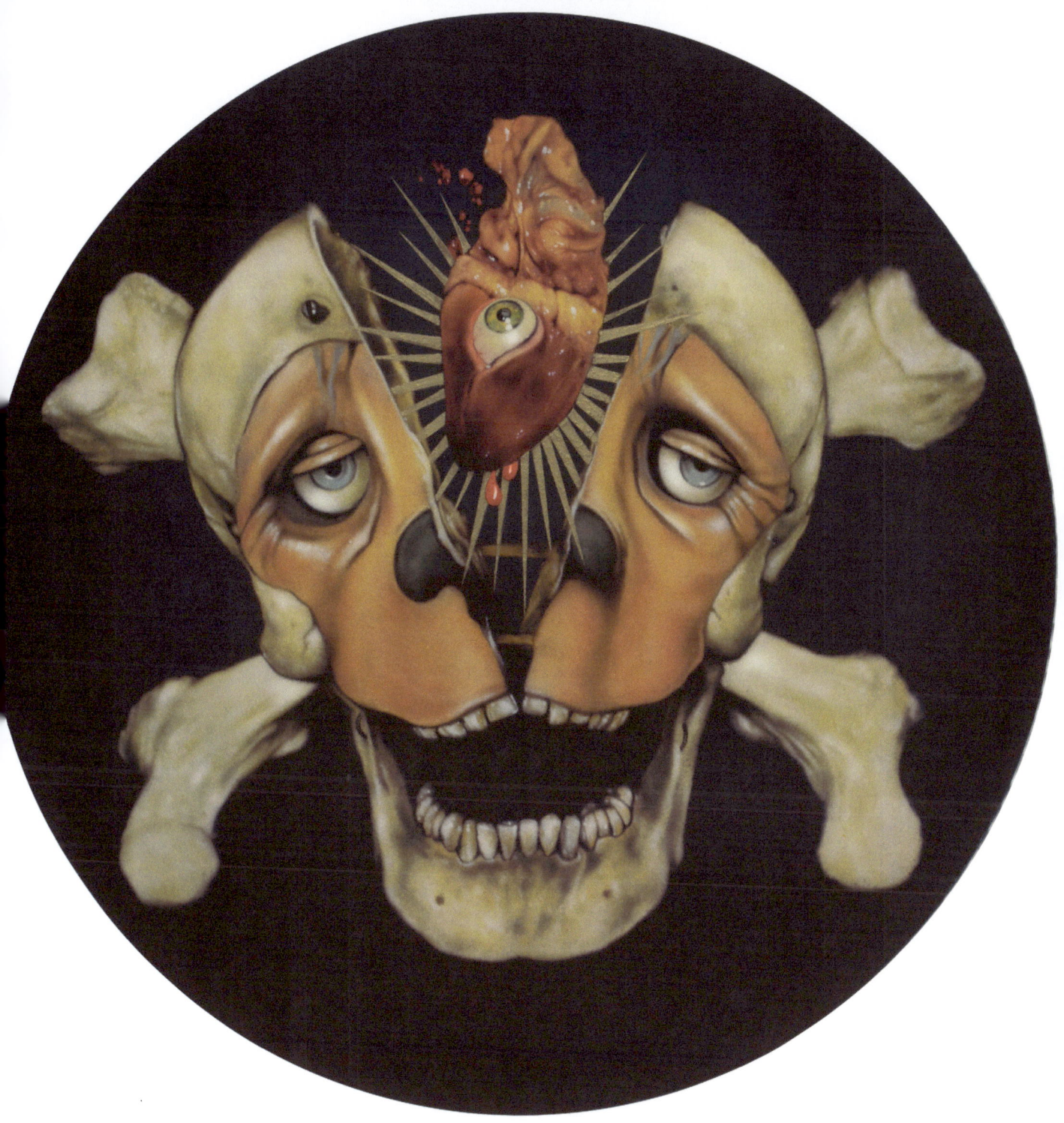

Rodrigo Cifuentes: *Forever Young*
Graphite and oil on paper, 23.5 x 17.5 cm

"Create images leaving aside concept over intellectualization, as simple as dancing to Alphaville's beat."

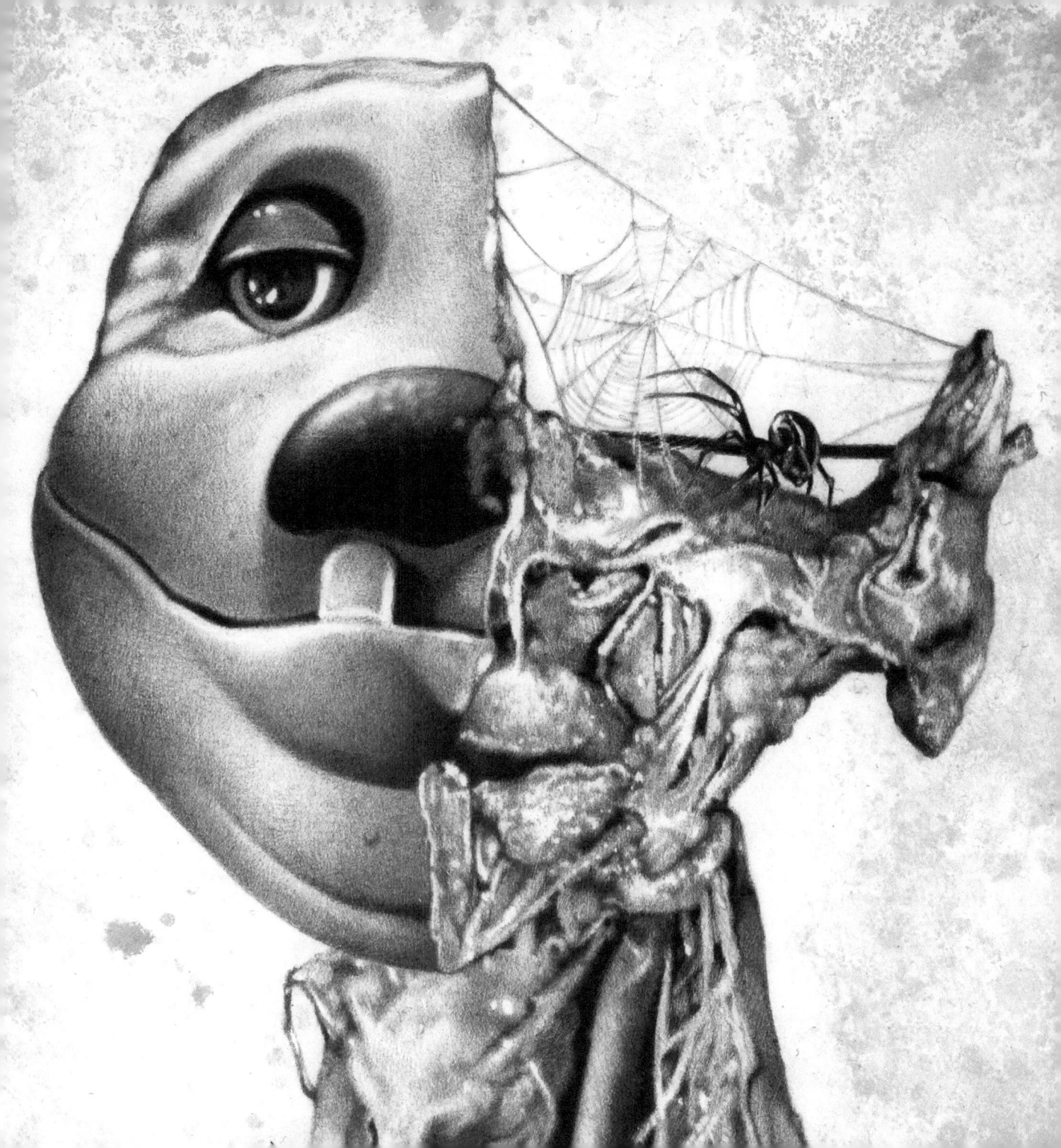

Mario Cinquemani

Cinquemani

Born on January 4th, 1982 in Guadalajara, Mario's artistic journey started with a training in figure drawing at the Art League of Houston, Texas. He enriched his knowledge with the renowned sculptor Willy Wang and a Misch Technique workshop given by New York based artist Bob Venosa. Mario Cinquemani followed his artistic pursuits to London and various cities in Europe, which finally gave birth to a life fully devoted to painting.

Evoking impressionist feelings with his colour palette and obsessive short brush-strokes, Mario has always aimed his technical aspirations towards the supremacy of colour and realism, achieving extremely detailed depictions of intimate projections from each of his characters' psyches – timeless and eye-pleasing characters and their scenarios, almost weightless and lost in the comprehension of their self-made environment. We are made to wonder if they are alive or if these depictions are the voyeuristic records of a murder.

Mario Cinquemani: *Testigo (Witness)*
Oil painting, 25.5 x 29 cm

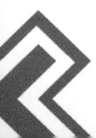

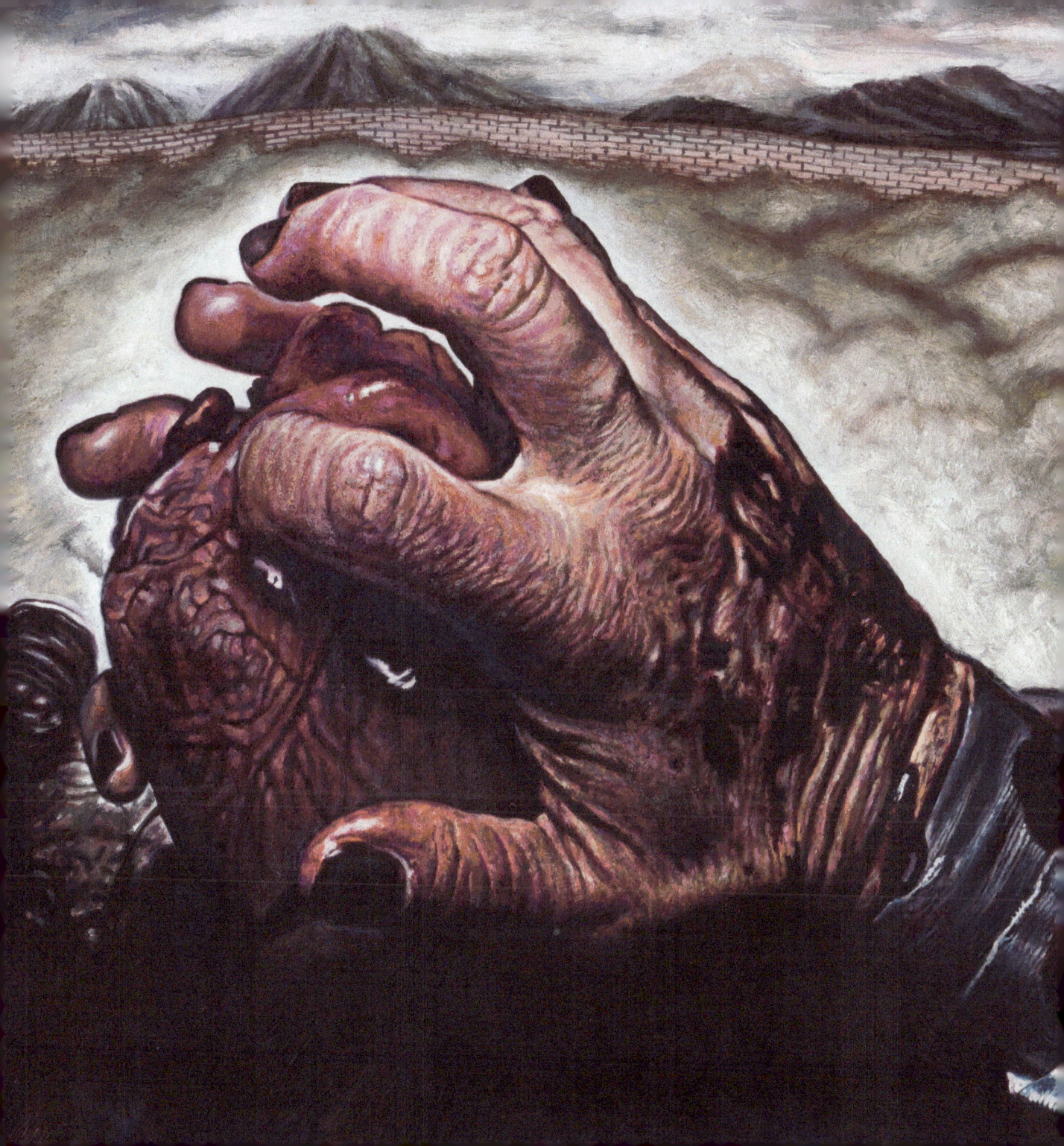

Mario Cinquemani: *Untitled*
Charcoal on paper, 28 x 37.5 cm

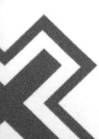

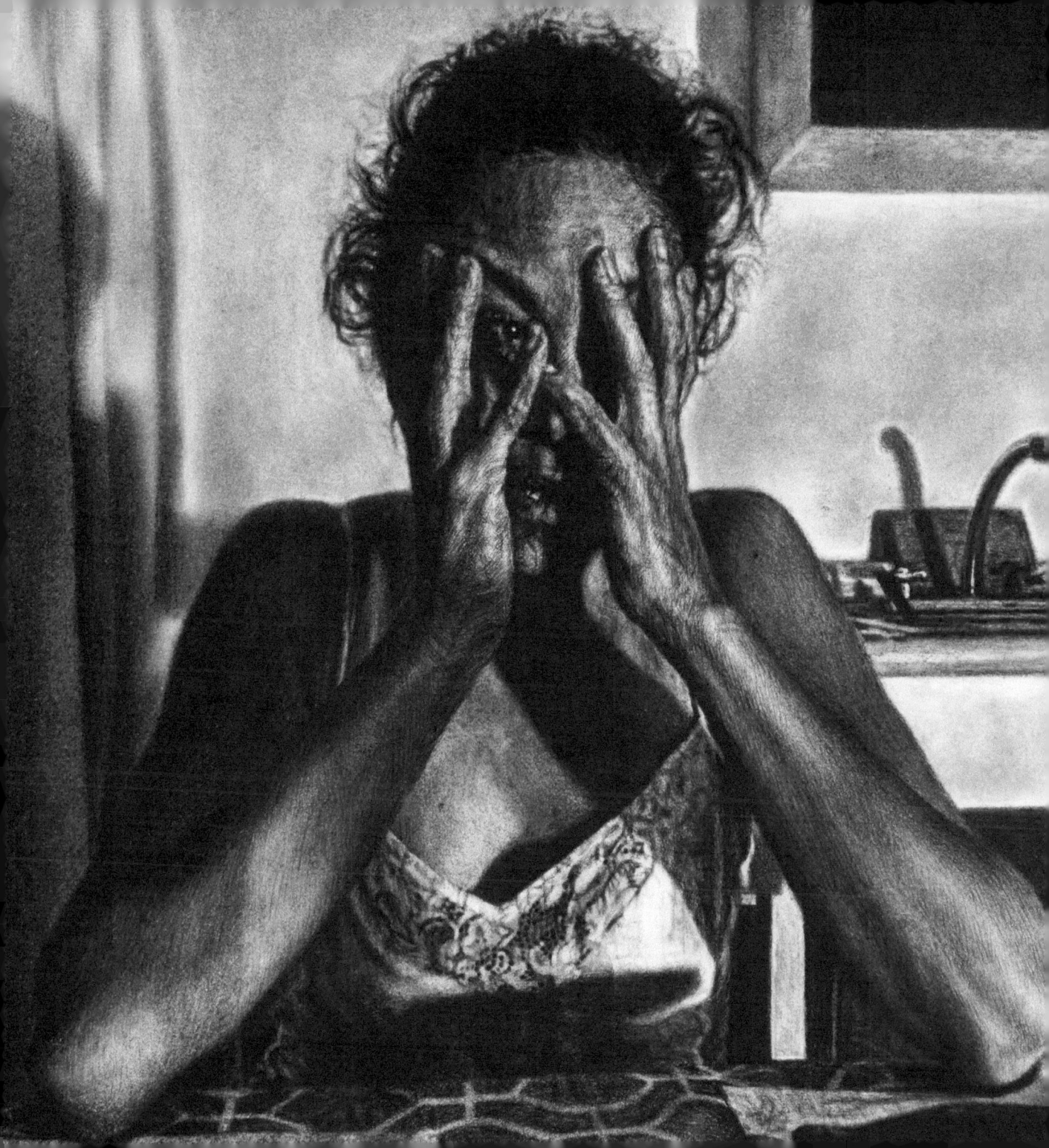

Ricardo Fernández

Born in 1971 in Durango, Mexico, Ricardo Fernandez Ortega's way of adding and subtracting light and carefully controlling rich, dark, luscious tones resembles great 17th-century Spanish masters such as Diego Velázquez. His intuitive chiaroscuro takes us to a mysterious, sometimes surreal space, where women wear elegant armour and extravagant headdresses and exist in empty terrains while participating in strange, fantastical and dream-like activities.

Through his usage of a historical style, Ortega authentically assembles an extended body of work that resembles and continues, in many ways, the legacy of the old Spanish masters. His curious themes may feel contemporary, but, overall, it is hard not to go back in time while enjoying these skilfully painted works.

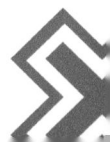

Ricardo Fernández: *Cyan*
Oil on canvas, 50 x 40 cm

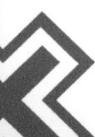

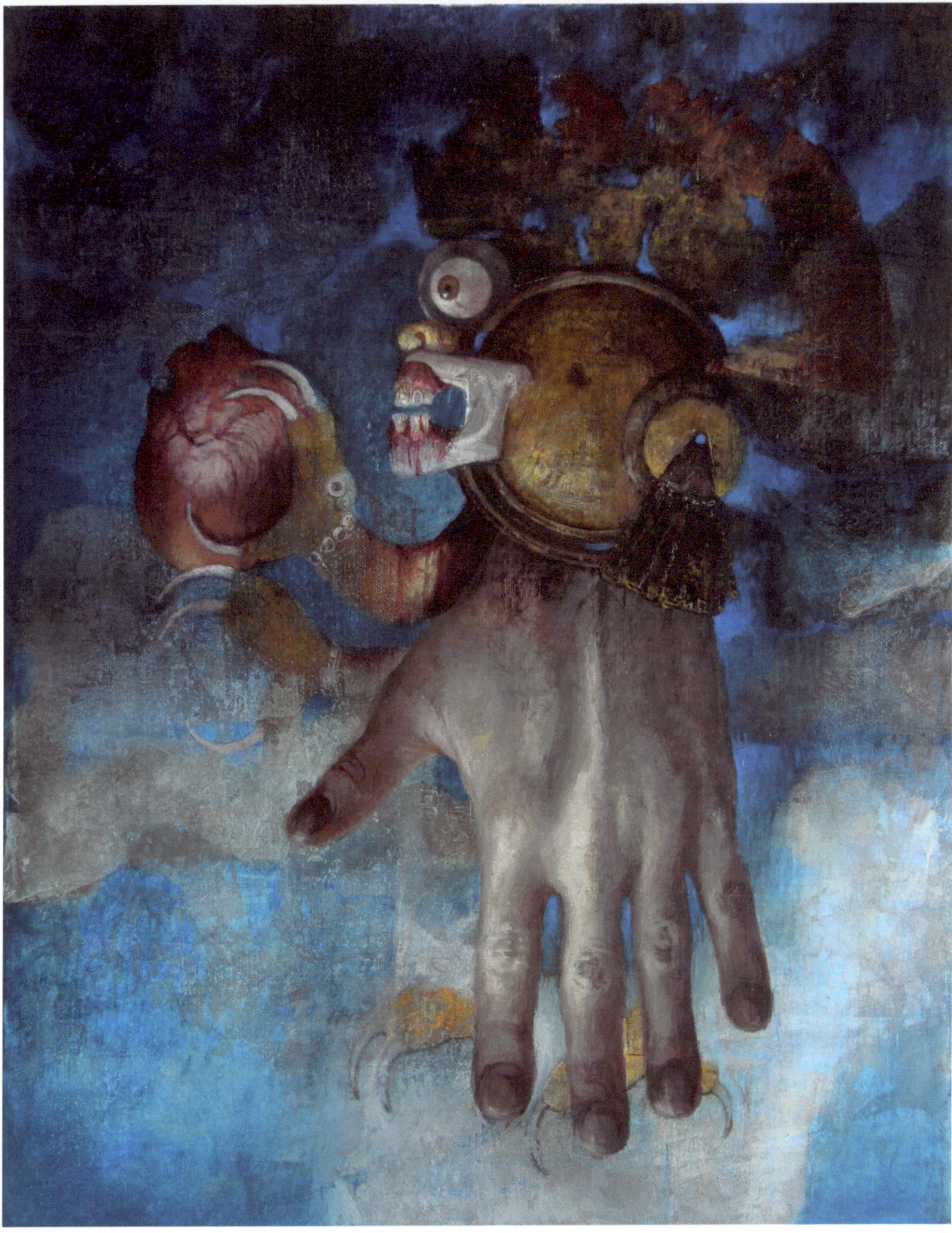

Ricardo Fernández: *Luz Perpetua (Perpetual Light)*
Oil on canvas, 50 x 40 cm

"A ceremonial knife used to extract the heart of the sacrificed, now wearing a suit and tie. We must offer hearts dripping with blood to the Gods, so that the light be perpetual. Before, the sun was that light, but today, that light is the economy."

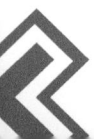

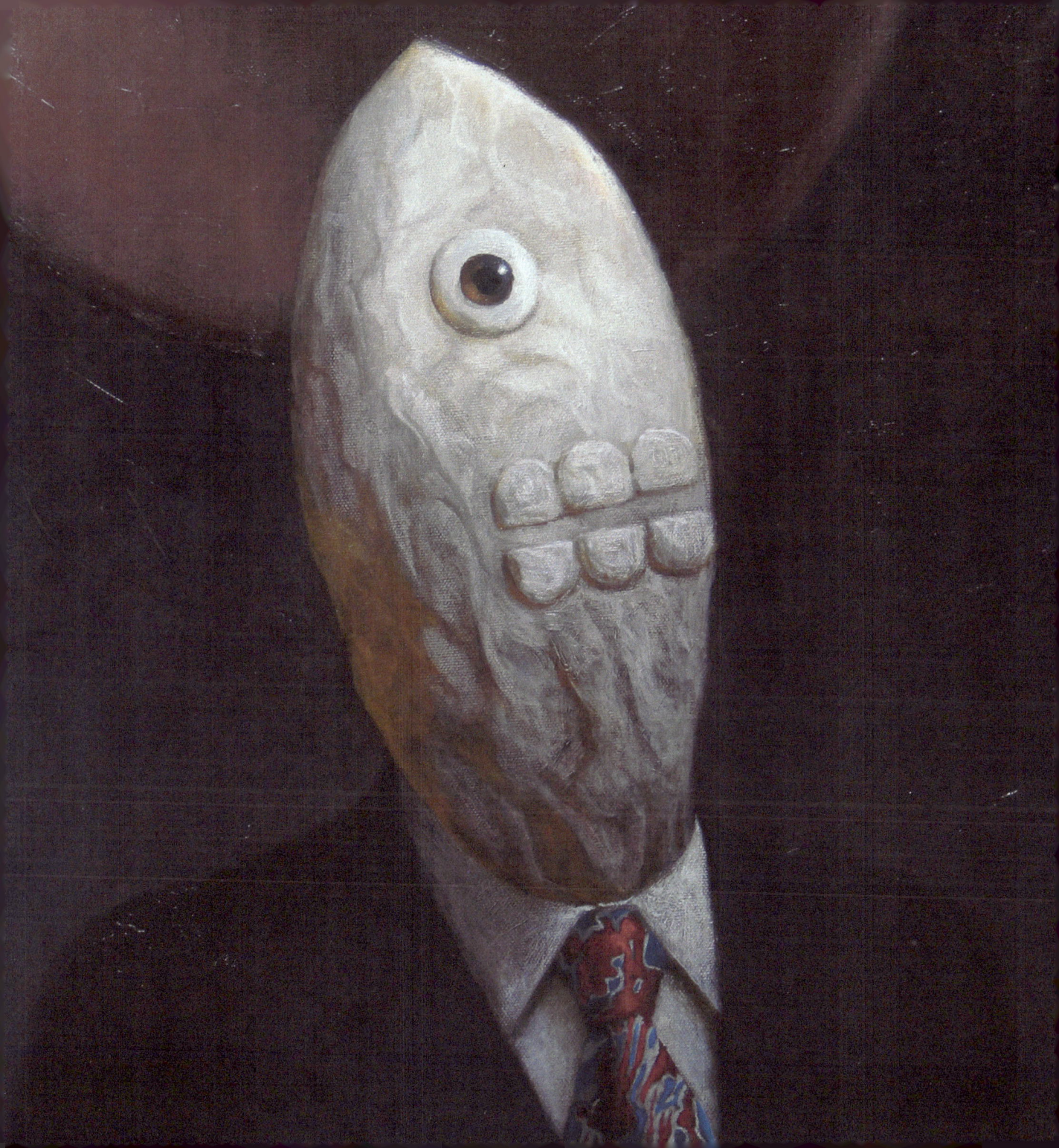

Victor Hugo Jácome

h. Jácome.

Born in Mexico City in 1982, Víctor Hugo Jácome is a self-taught artist who developed his artistic knowledge by observation and strict practice. Just like Rembrandt and Van Gogh, Víctor Hugo Jácome works with elements that are close at hand, finding beauty and poetry in what is usually ignored or seen as too ordinary by the majority.

The passage of time and its effects on the day-by-day is what drives Víctor Hugo to return these forgotten objects into the sacred world of art. He provides the audience with a tangible world that's usually hidden, like a ghost of humankind in a world where there is no longer a human presence, only its remnants. However, this world of solitude is never hopeless, as it somehow gives a comfortable feeling of rest and contemplative joy.

Victor Hugo Jácome: *Untitled*
Oil on canvas on board, 30 x 50 cm

"This artwork approaches death through its different suggestive aspects, like the coexistence of calmness within harshness, where the lifeless breathes through the painting, a silent death scream in a quiet atmosphere, and a recently arrived absence that compels you to be here, in a suspended time."

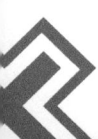

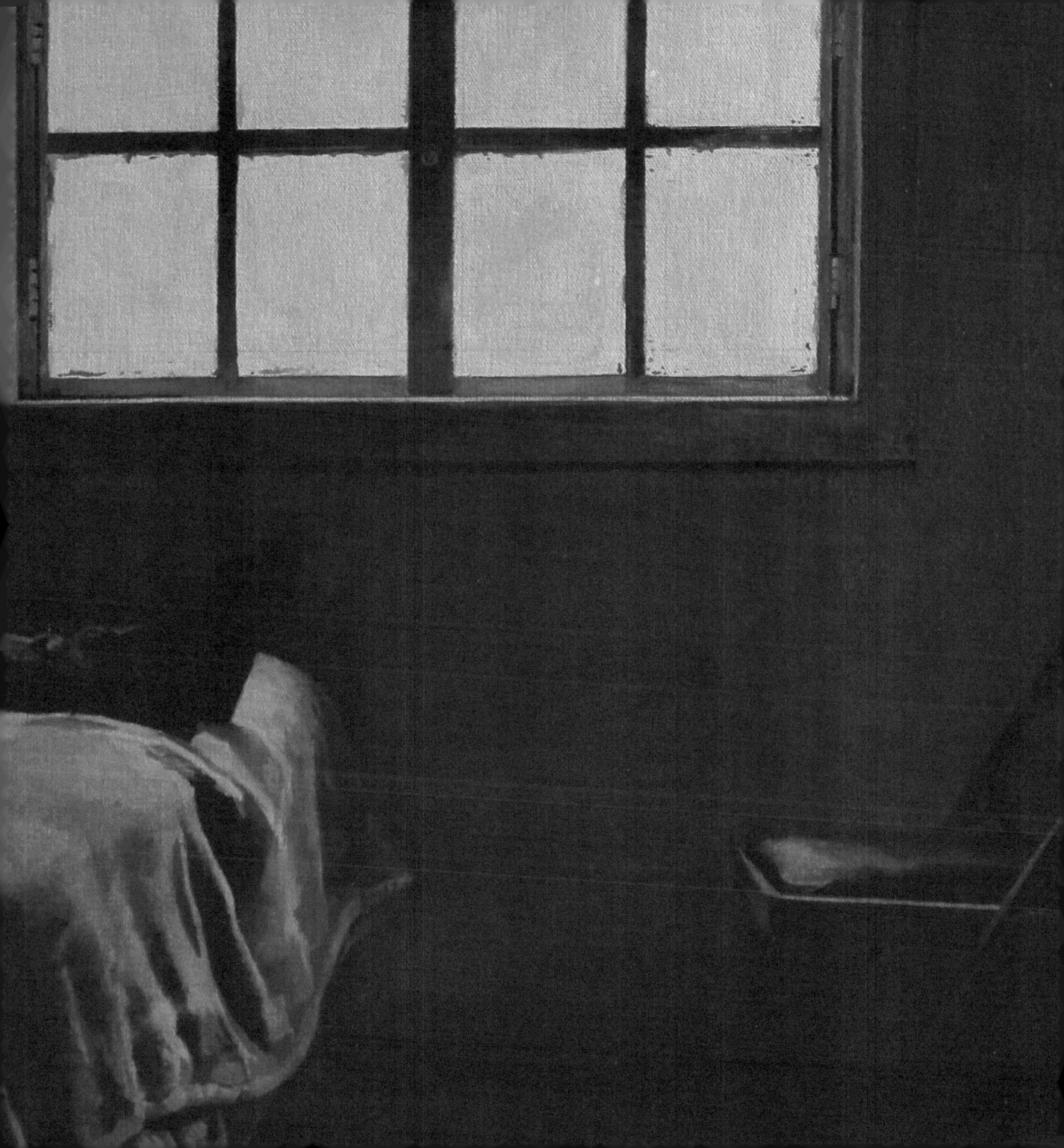

Victor Hugo Jácome: *Play*
Oil on canvas on board, 30 x 35 cm

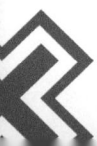

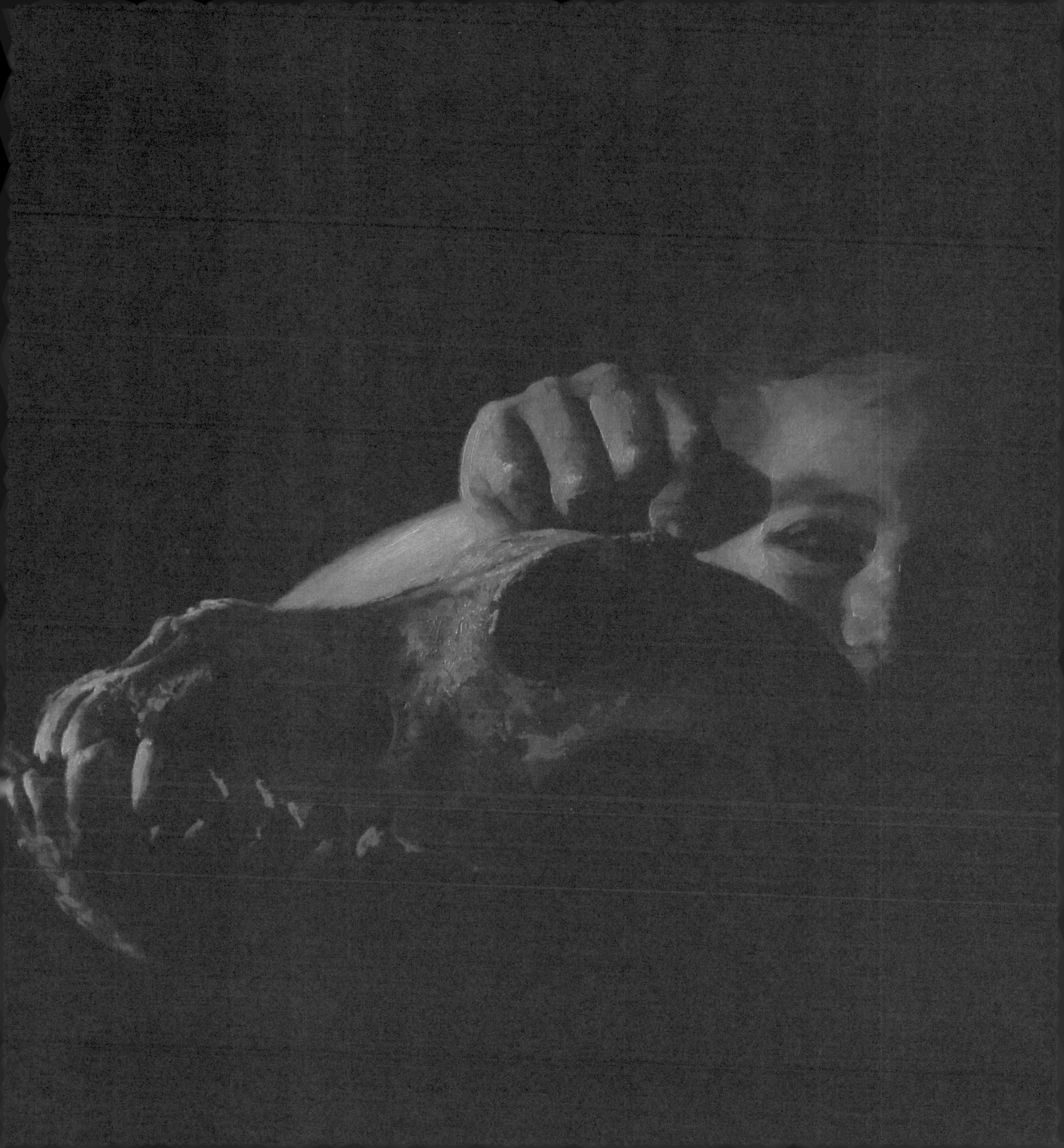

José Luis López Galván

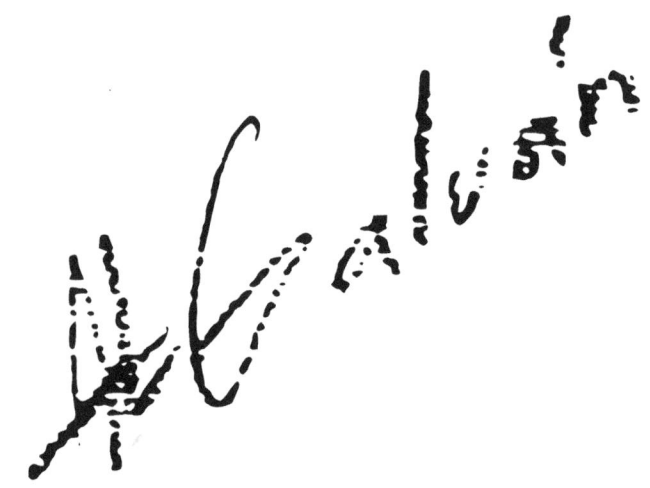

Born in the city of Guadalajara, Jalisco, in 1985, after focusing on graphic design studies at the University of Guadalajara, José Luis López Galván was later seduced by oil painting, in which he currently works almost completely. An admirer of the Baroque and of Rembrandt's chiaroscuro, and of the inventiveness of painters like Salvador Dalí or Remedios Varo, little by little he is creating his own symbolism.

At the beginning, in an empirical way, he used visual media to communicate different concepts like death, fear or hypocrisy, using without limitations animal characters, humans or objects. The main goal of his work is the creation of a collage that, when integrated, will represent a believable portrait of the world: not just of the way that things look, but of their scent.

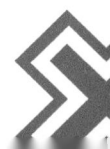

José Luis López Galván: *Amor y Miedo (Love and Fear)*
Oil on canvas, 50 x 40 cm

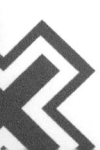

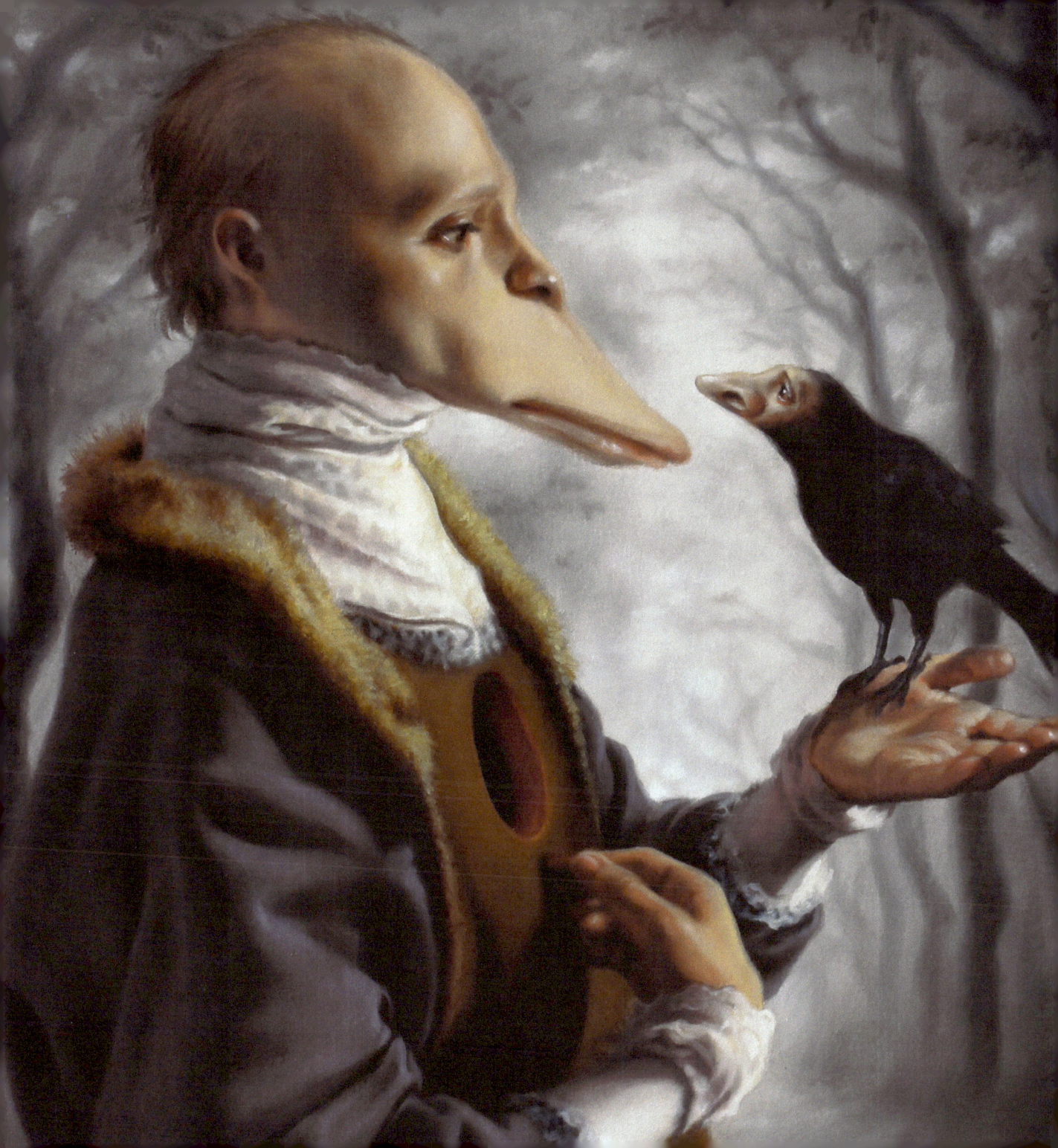

José Luis López Galván: *Cabeza de Santo (Head of a Saint)*
Oil on canvas, 50 x 50 cm

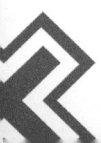

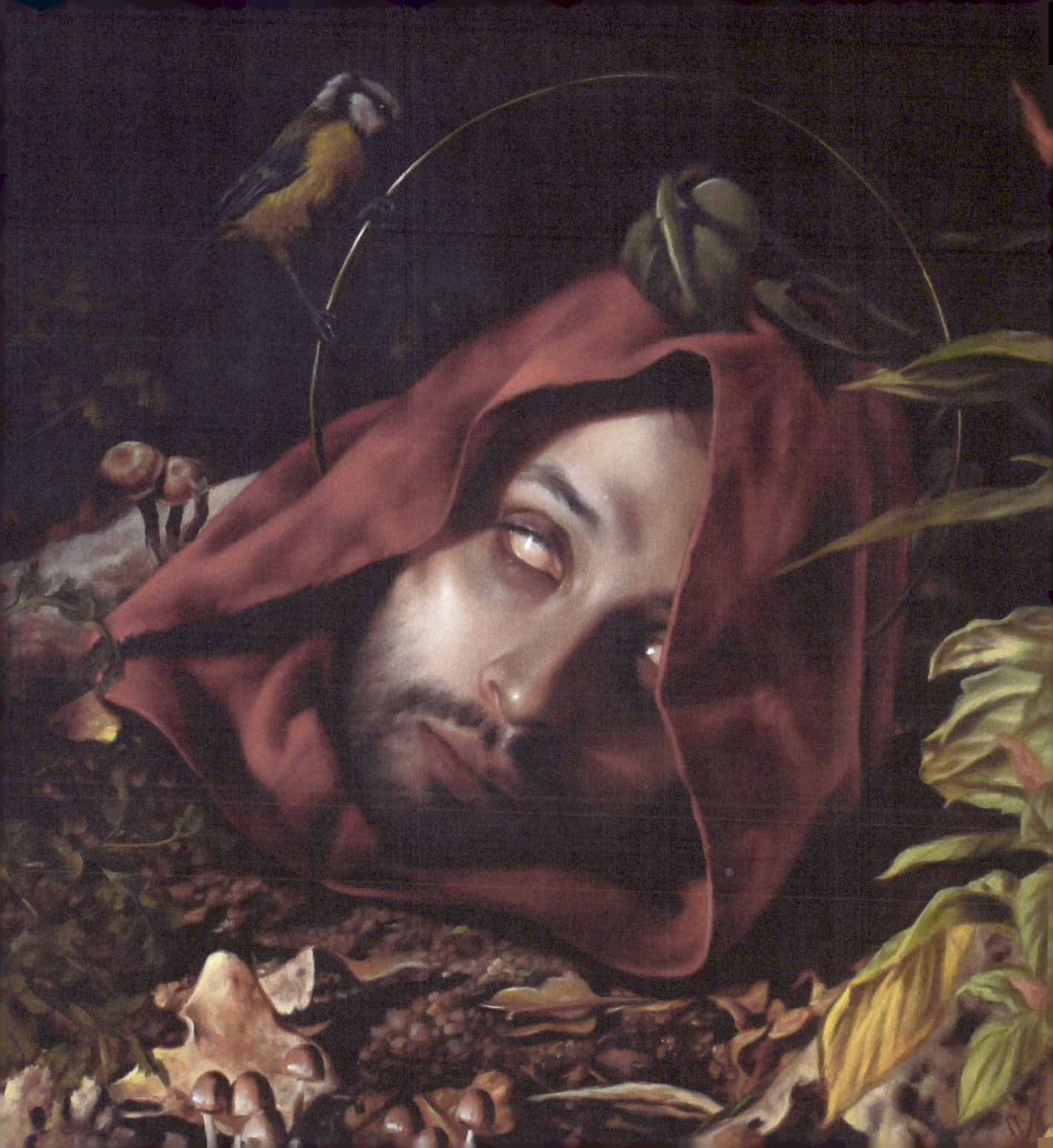

Patrick Mallow

A heavy metal fan, a painter who also thinks of himself as a rock star. His paintings express the passion he has for heavy metal and for his favourite actors, taking it to the level of a fetish: it's his way of narrowing the distance between him and his idols.

Peter Nagle (1974) is an Irish artist who took his pen name from the patron saint of the Catholic boarding school where he completed his primary education ("St. Patrick's") and Mallow, his hometown. He had a strictly Catholic education during his childhood (a visible influence on his work), and emigrated to London in his teens, where he worked as a butcher's assistant until the publication of his first work in an independent rock magazine. His first work recognised in the art circuit is "Necrophilia" (1998); paintings based on stills of bloody scenes from commercial cinema. His work is known more widely as "Fanatic from hell" (2004-2008), which earned him entrance to the Saatchi gallery in London, one of the most important art venues in the world.

(Peter Nagle / Patrick Mallow is a fictional character created by Javier Pulido Gándara as part of an art performance.)

Patrick Mallow: *Lucky Charms*
Acrylic on paper, 29 x 29 cm

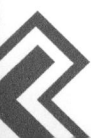

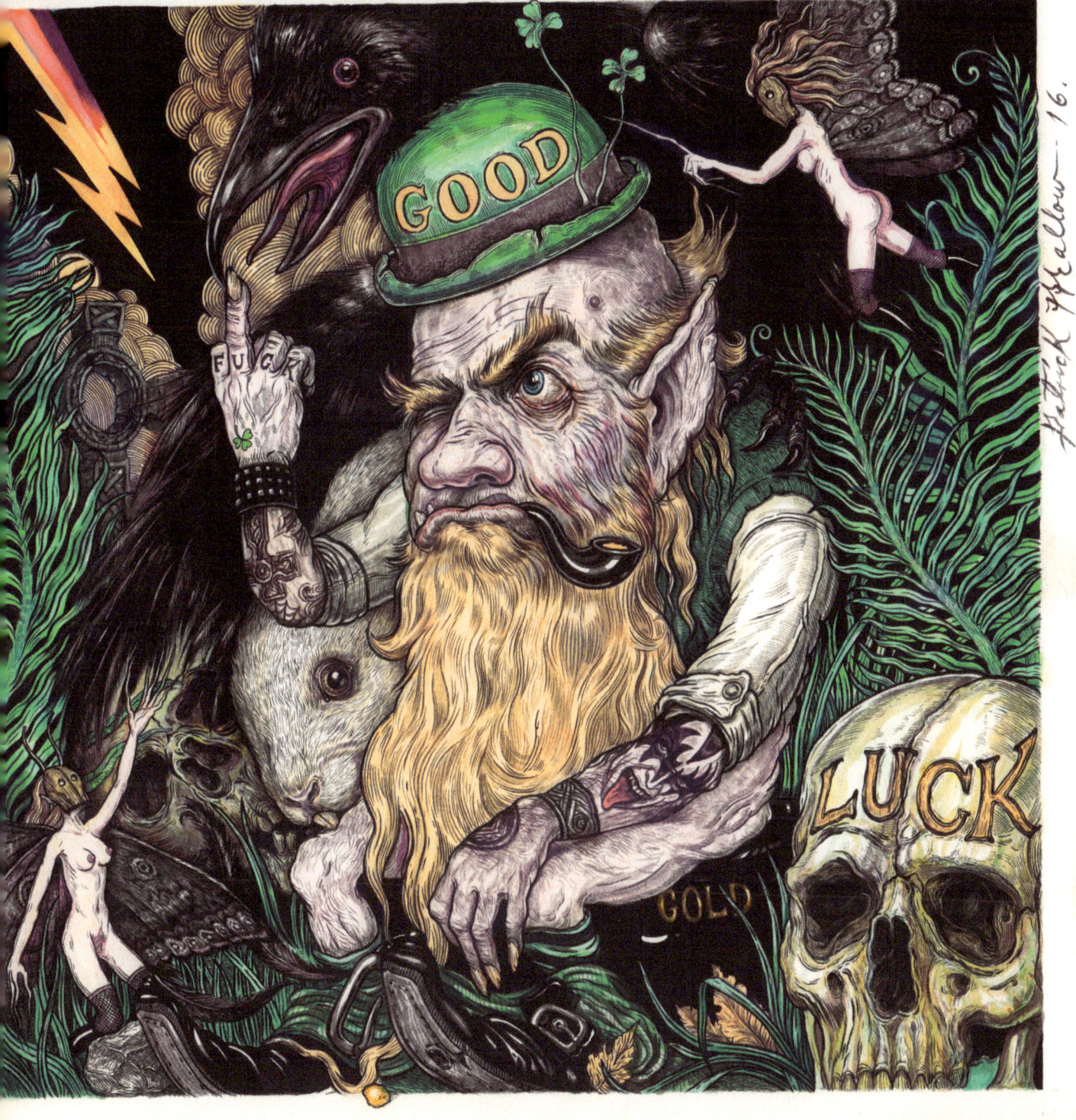

Román Miranda

Román miranda

Born in Mexico City in 1973, this established Mexican artist graduated in graphic design at the Universidad Iberoamericana in Mexico City. His passion for the fine arts was born after his first experiments with engraving at San Miguel de Allende, Mexico.

After giving up his graphic design career in the 2000s, Román devoted himself completely to the artistic profession and freely faced the world with his own personal inquisitiveness about life. His technical tendencies are inclined to realism in drawing, etching, or mixed media, sometimes as figures fading into impeccable dream-like blank backgrounds and at times as figures stabbed or beheaded by violent and expressive loud colours.

His artworks are always an invitation to an introspective journey by the hand of the artist, the rediscovery of ourselves, the deep communion with our emotional scars, the lonely journey of self-transformation and personal growth.

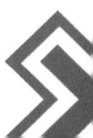

Román Miranda: *Empty Whispers I*
Oil and charcoal on board, 25 x 50 cm

Profound silence,
echoes of wind
carrying empty memories.

Rocks from childhood
in my pockets.

Slowly,
a forest of grass
growing as shadows
caressing my guts.

Lying here
fulfilled by void beats.

Eyes wide open,
then
again
a profound silence.

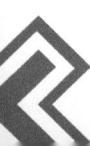

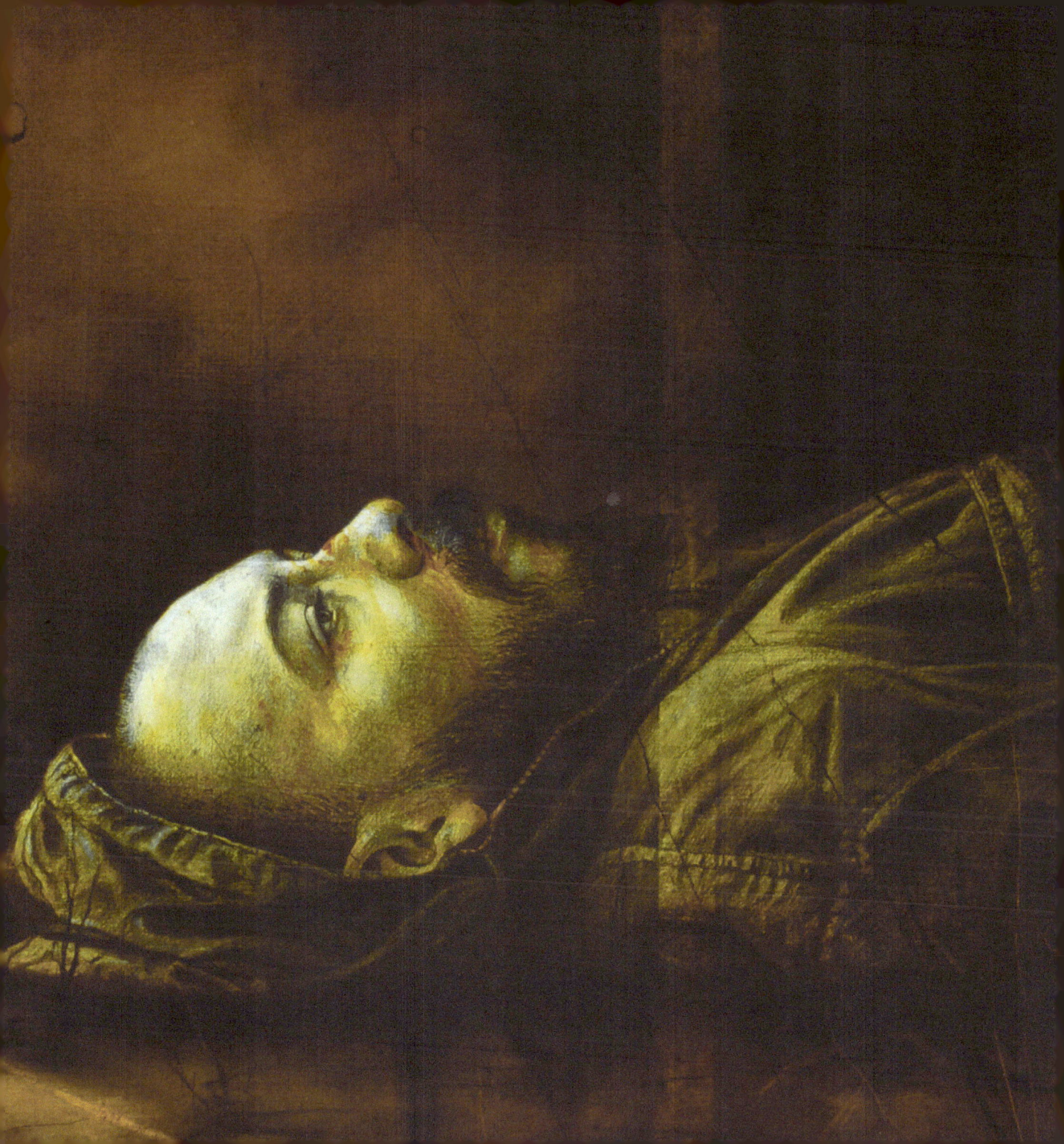

Román Miranda: *Empty Whispers II*
Oil and charcoal on board, 25 x 50 cm

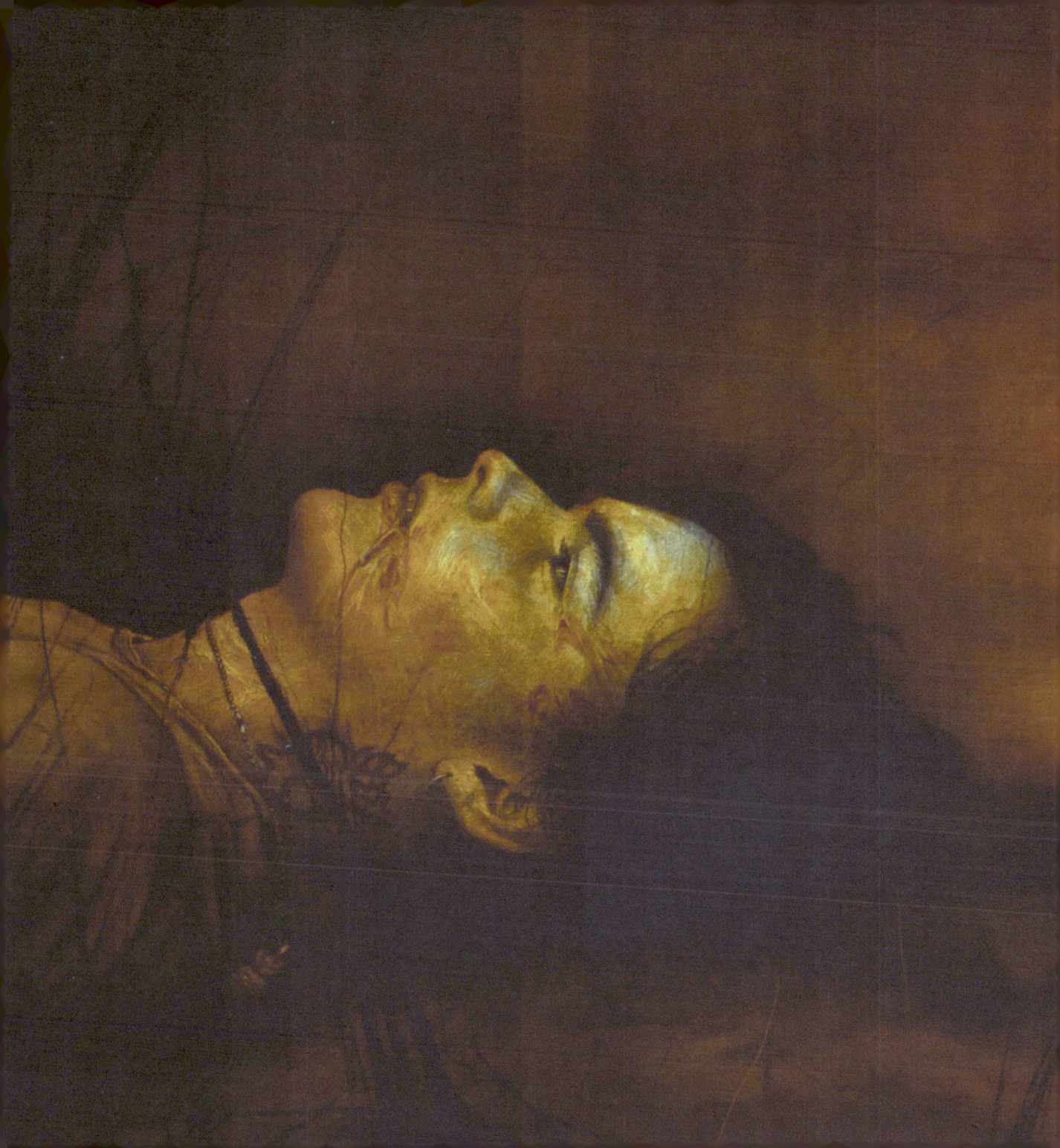

Rafael Rodríguez

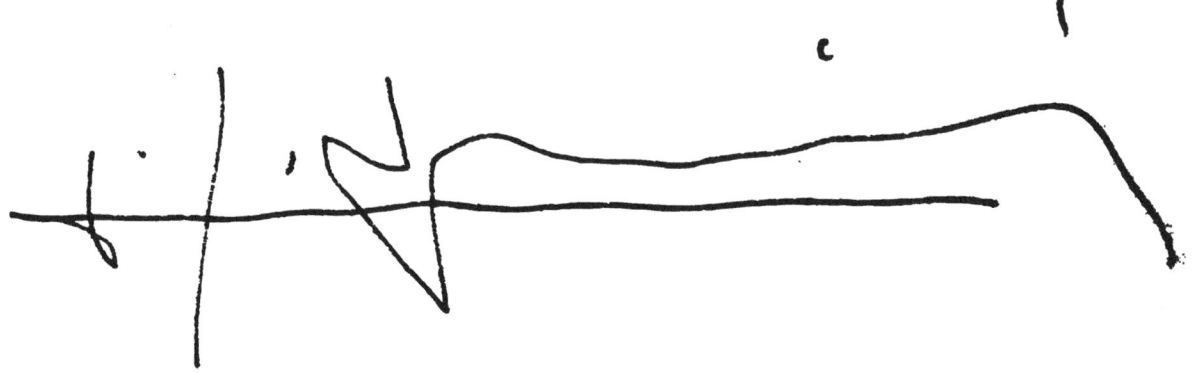

Born in Querétaro, México in 1977, Rafael Rodríguez is an architect who has been devoted to the visual arts since 1998. His work has been presented in museums and galleries in México, the United Kingdom, Canada, the United States, Spain, Sweden, and Austria. In 2006, his series of paintings Models for a Self-Portrait was presented at the National Portrait Gallery in London, and won second place for the gallery's annual prize. His portraits often try to represent the affection that the human face both simultaneously reflects and tries to hold back.

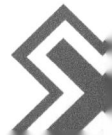

Rafael Rodríguez: *Obituario I (Obituary I)*
Oil on board, 22 x 27 cm

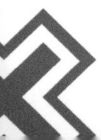

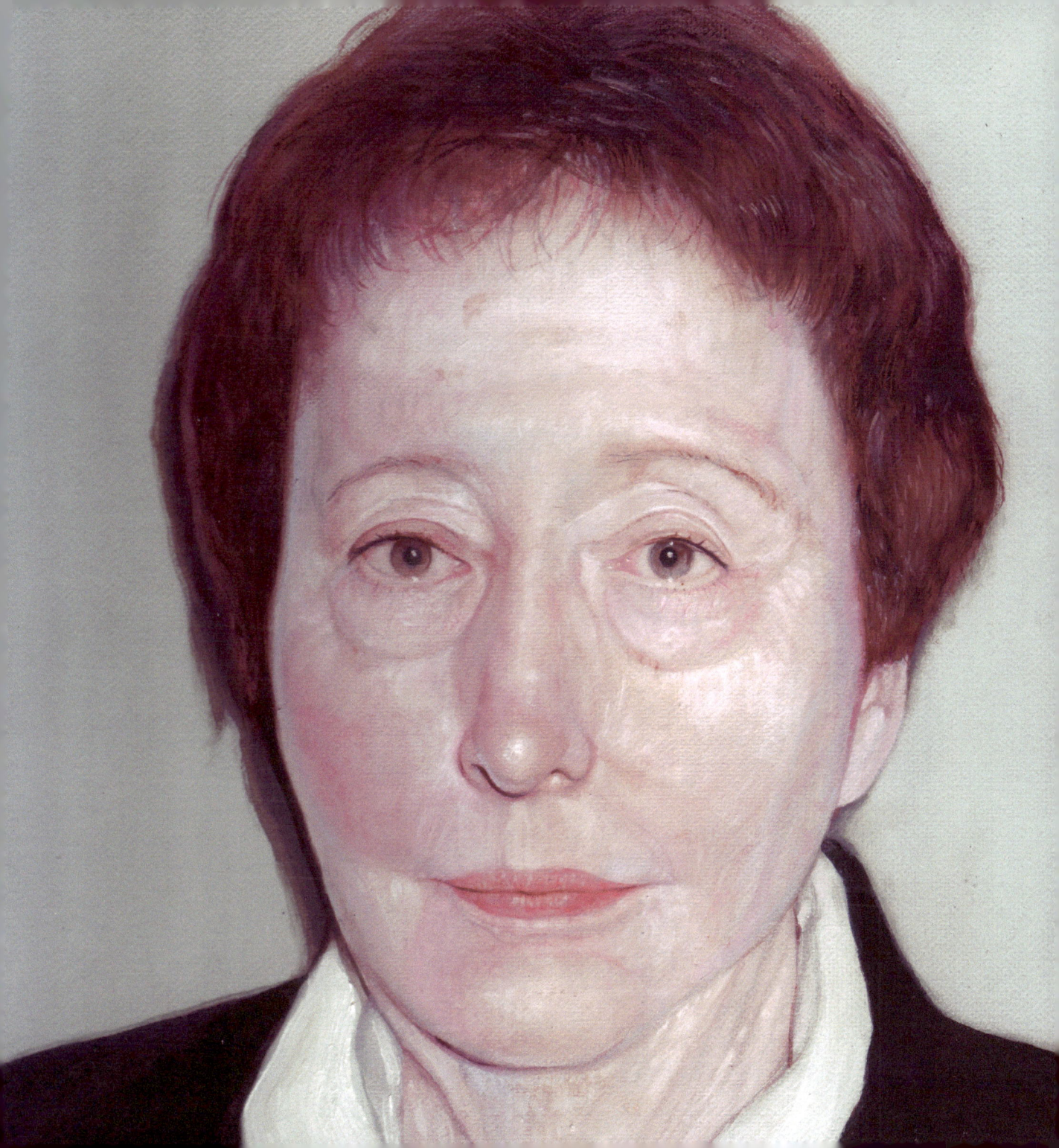

Rafael Rodríguez: *Obituario II (Obituary II)*
Oil on board, 22 x 27 cm

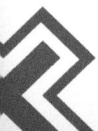

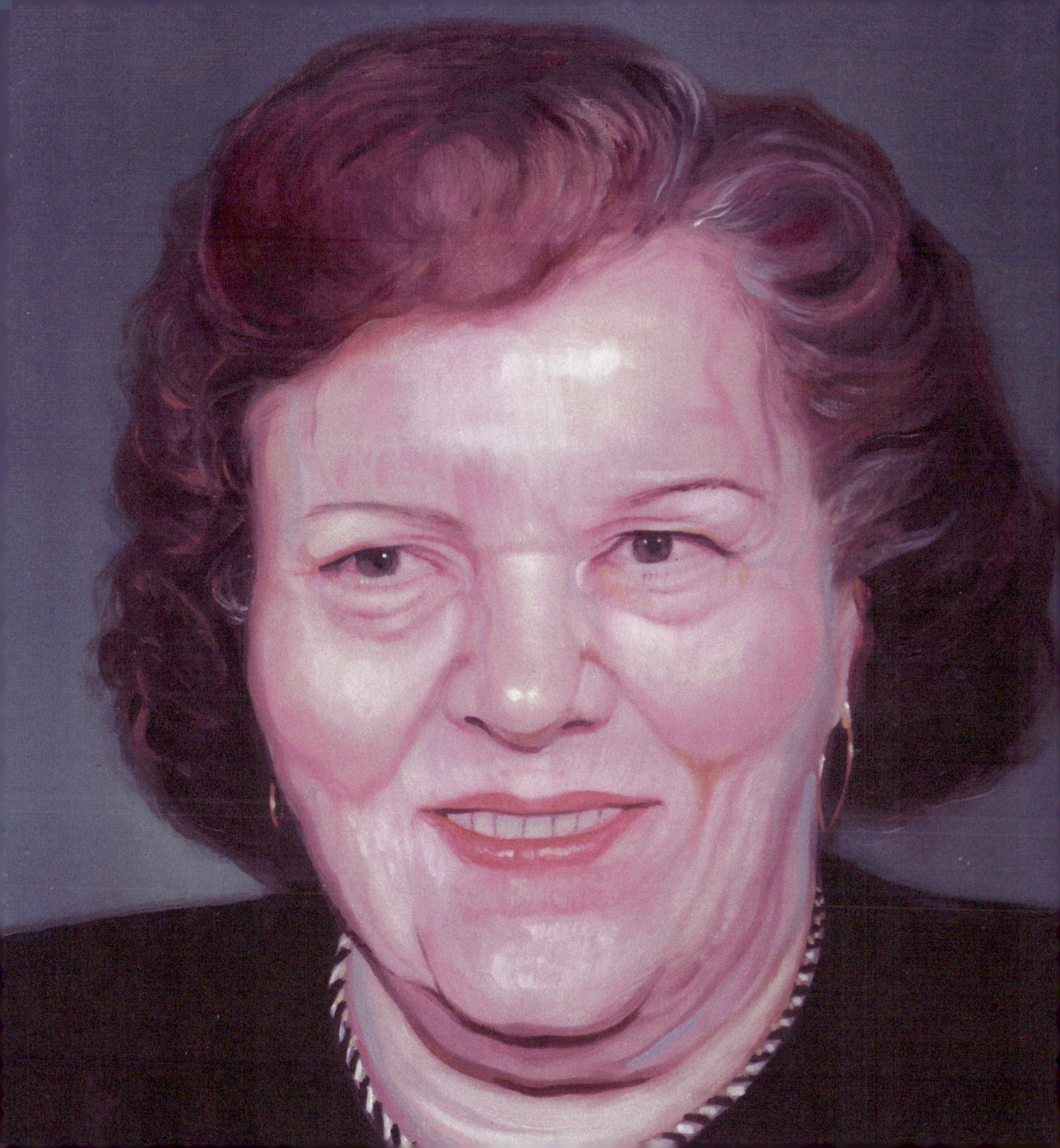

Rafael Rodríguez: *Obituario III (Obituary III)*
Oil on board, 22 x 27 cm

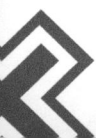

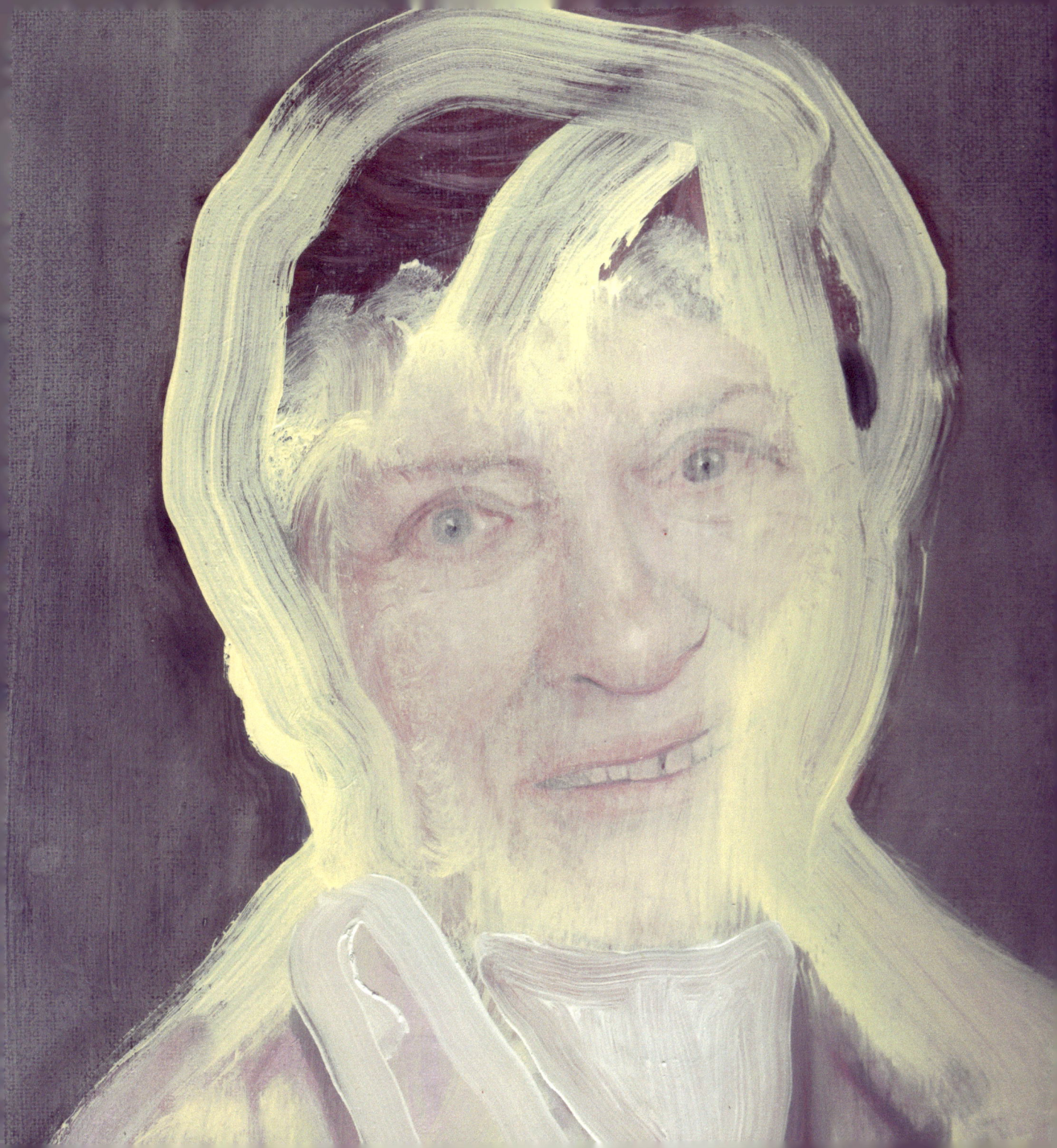

Rolando Sosa

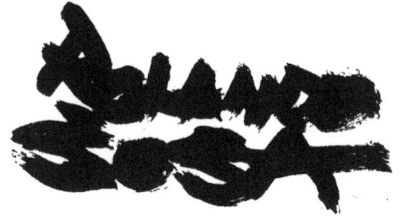

Born in Mexico City, 1983, Rolando earned a BFA in Illustration at the National School of Plastic Arts, UNAM, and later enriched his fine art knowledge at several schools and private fine art courses in Mexico. Rolando Sosa aims his artistic intentions towards the viewer with the certainty that painting can somehow pierce the depths of the soul. Loneliness and the obscurity of introspection are what emerge from the clean, expressive paintings of Rolando, where intimate closed landscapes absorb all light and warmth, and where an uncomfortable silence is all that remains.

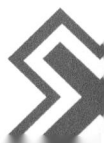

Rolando Sosa: *Quiebre y Mayólica (Fracture and Tiles)*
Oil on linen on wood, 35 x 35 cm

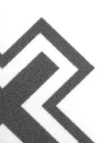

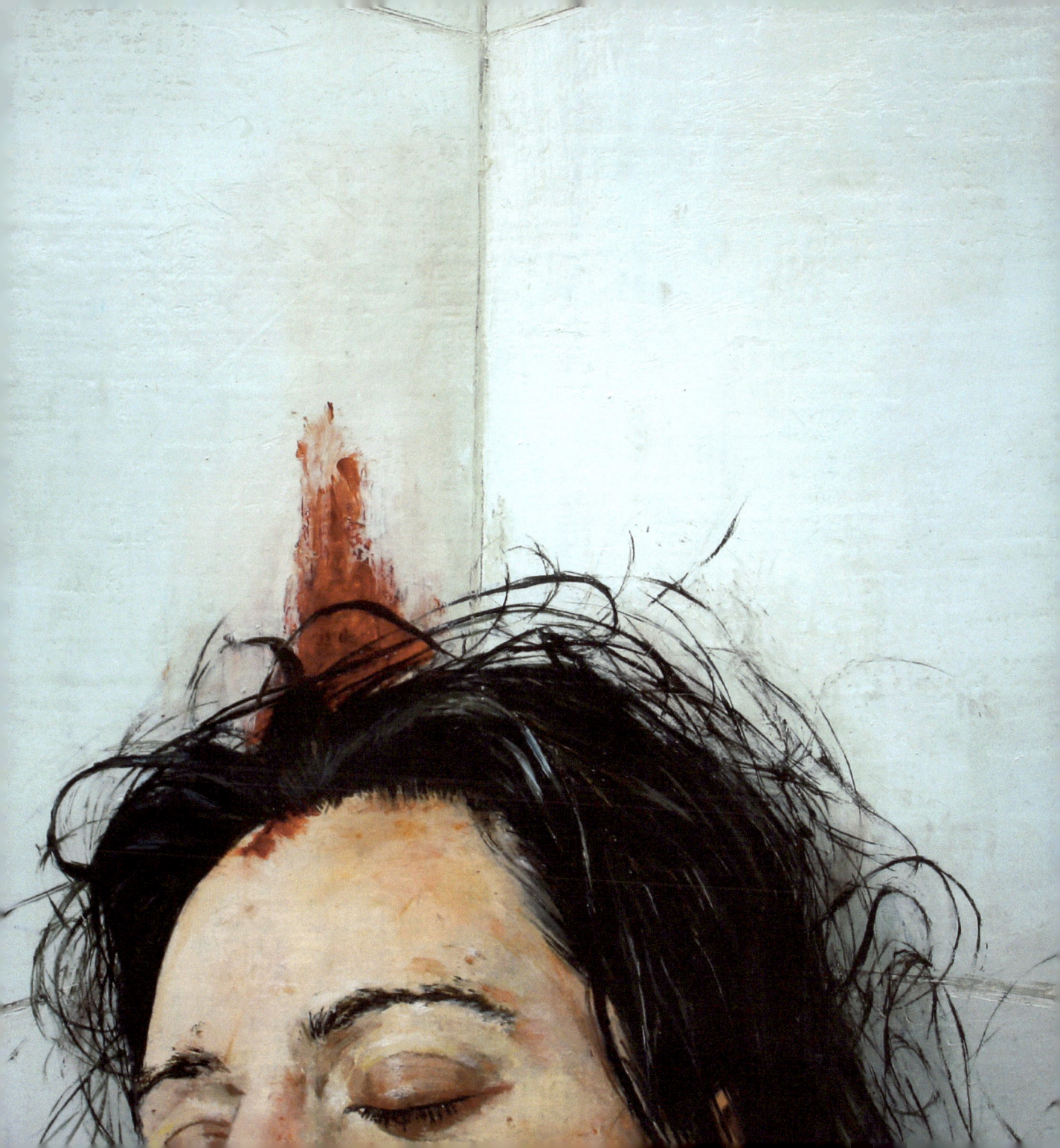

Rolando Sosa: *Ablación (Excision)*
Oil on linen on wood, 35 x 35 cm

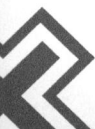

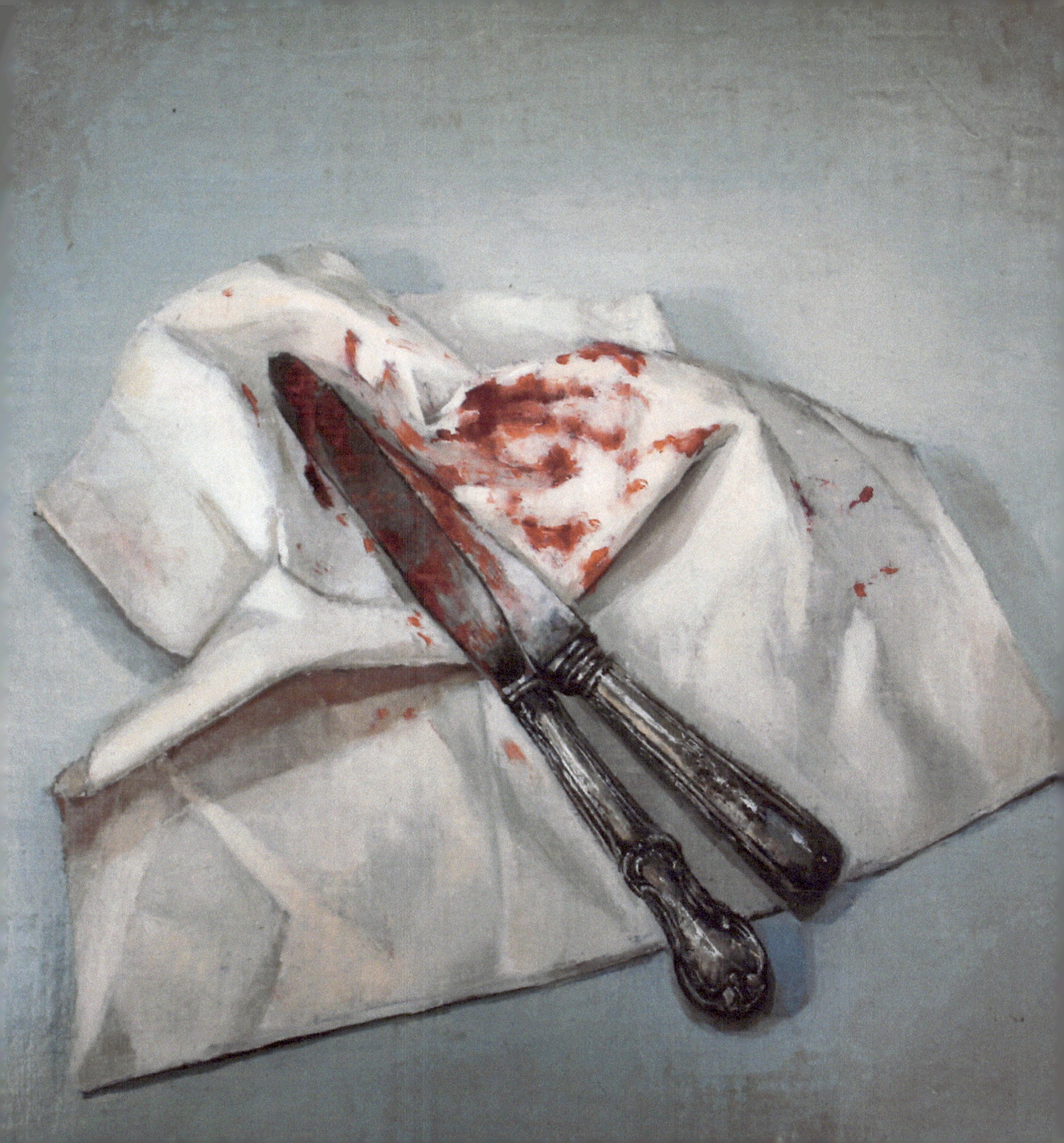

Talía Yañez

Born in Mexico City in 1980, Talía had a very broad academic development during the early years of her career, starting with a BFA degree in Visual Arts from the National School of Fine Arts in Mexico (ENAP) and continuing with various seminars on cinema, Mexican prehistoric art, etc.

A versatile artist whose artistic path led to involvement in makeup design, set design and murals, among other fields, she later focused her career on fine art and realism. Inspired by the symbolic language of the XVII century, now translated into a contemporary narrative, Talía often depicts scenarios where the mundane unravels with the theatricality of life, not as an incidental record, but as a crystallised glimpse of our existence that invites viewers to analyse and emotionally sympathise with their own human condition.

Talía Yañez: *Flyman*
Conte on drafting film, 30 x 22 cm

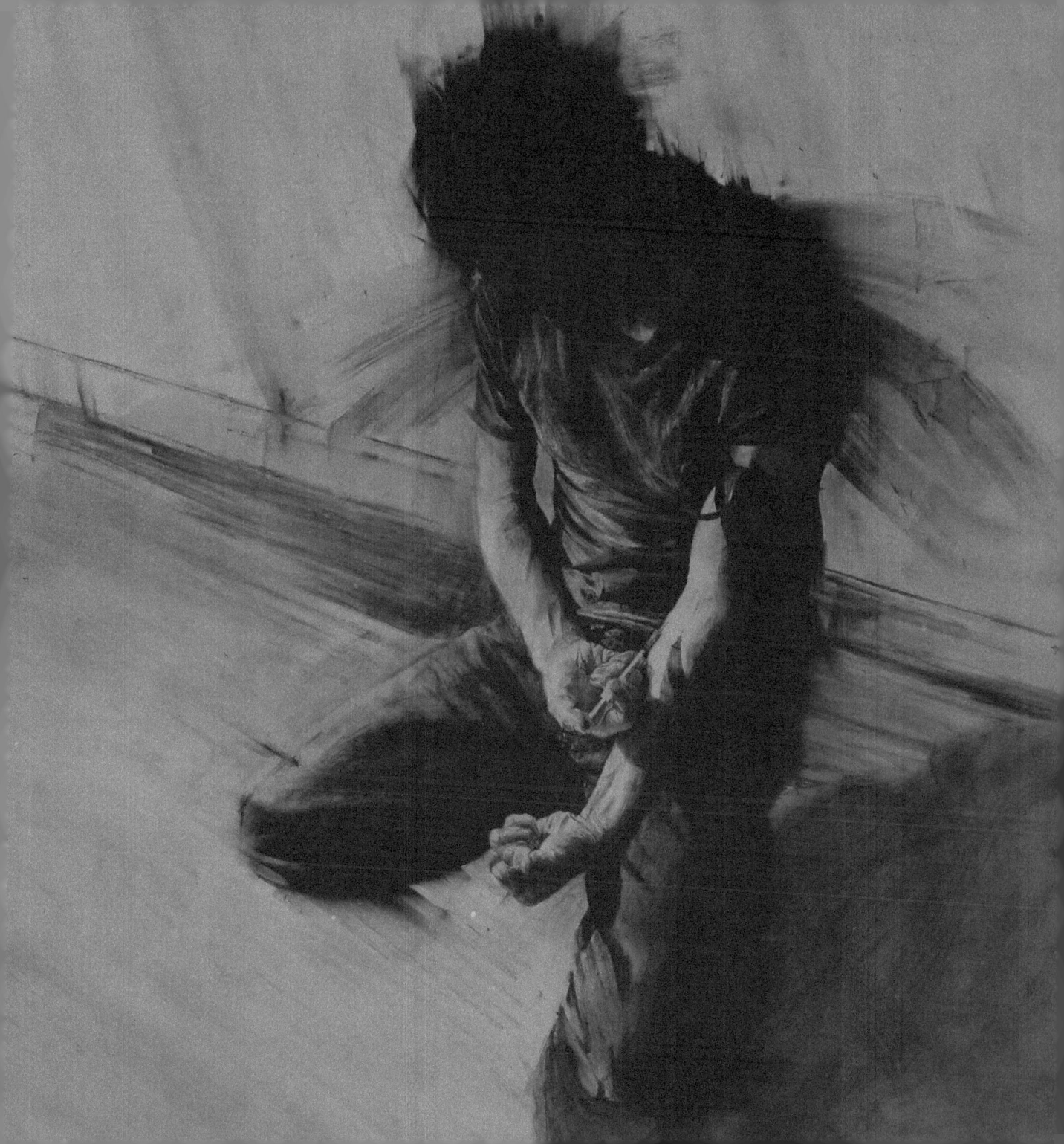

Talía Yañez: *Metallic Taste*
Oil on canvas, 40 x 50 cm

"... decay, misery, putrefaction, slavery, all veiled by illusion, our voracious hunger for distraction and palliatives keeps us hypnotized, denying our own mortality, the state of our flesh doomed to rot; we live with complacency (it isn´t about resignation) while beaten by reality, sometimes we only perceive a slight funny metallic taste, no big deal..."

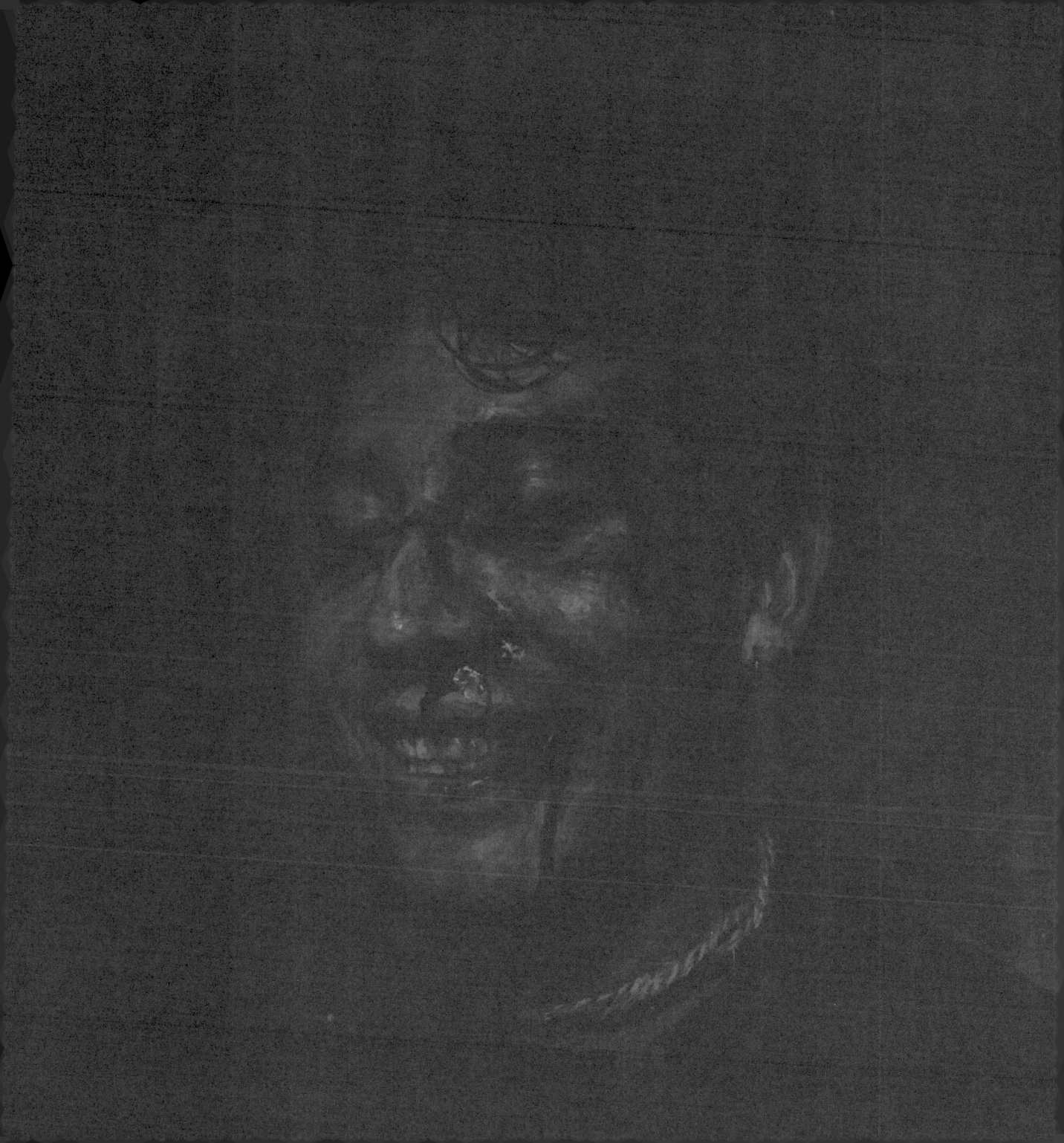

Kikyz1313

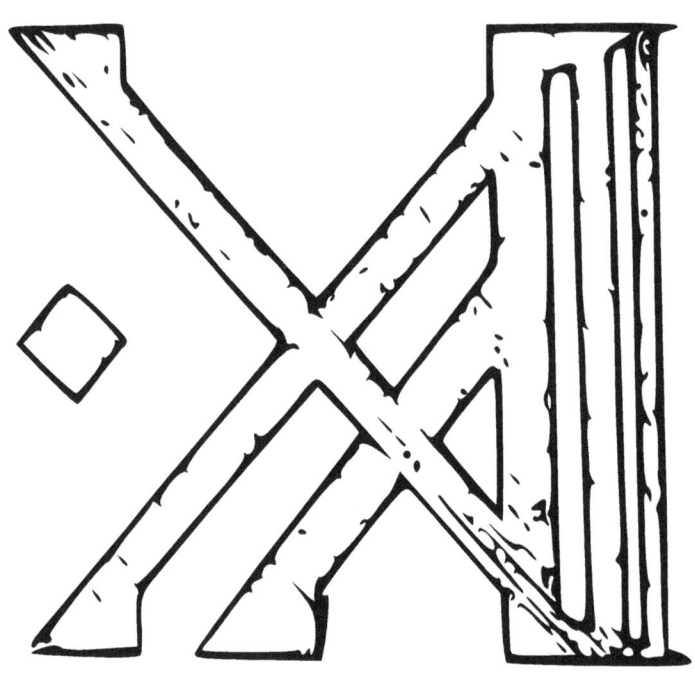

Born in 1988 in Querétaro, México as Laura Lucía Ferrer Zamudio, Kikyz1313 adopted her artistic name after her BFA in Fine Art at Querétaro State University.

Her visual histories have been showcased in several art fairs and group shows around the U.S.A. and Europe and promise to keep reconfiguring our perception of life in several venues in the near future.

Kikyz1313's artworks are known for creating a new aesthetic where the bizarre or the strange coexist with the paradigms of beauty inside intricate scenarios of gloom and death.

The human condition and society's behavioural contradictions are the subject matters she likes to depict in her graphite atmospheres, where the tenderness of childhood narrates the flaws, failures and raw nature of humankind.

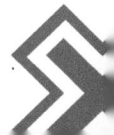

Kikyz1313: *True Love Shredded by Conflict*
Graphite, watercolour and pastel on paper mounted on board, 33 x 26 cm

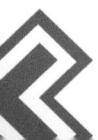

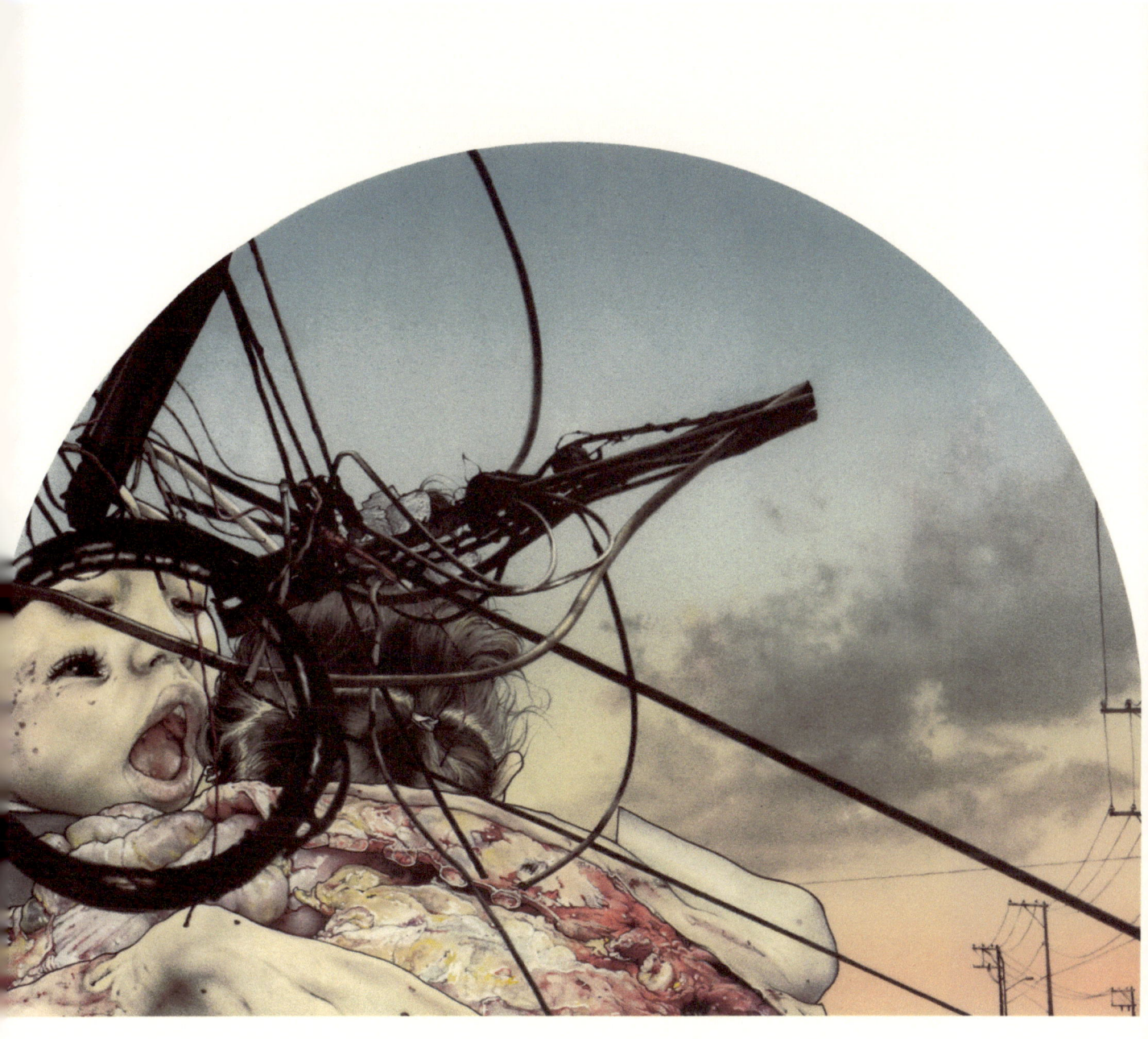

For the preparation of this catalogue
the publishers are grateful
to a number of anonymous donors,
and to Lisette Gebhardt, Miguel Ferrer,
and María Guadalupe Zamudio Alfaro.